Mary Said What She Said

DARRYL PINCKNEY

Mary Said What She Said

Commissioned by Robert Wilson

faber

First published in 2024
by Faber and Faber Limited
The Bindery, 51 Hatton Garden, London ECIN 8HN
Typeset by Agnesi Text, Hadleigh, Suffolk
Printed in England by CPI Group (UK) Ltd, Croydon CRO 4YY

A CIP record for this book is available from the British Library

ISBN 978–0–571–39316–9

Printed and bound in the UK on FSC® certified paper in line with our continuing
commitment to ethical business practices, sustainability and the environment.
For further information see faber.co.uk/environmental-policy

2 4 6 8 10 9 7 5 3 1

Mary Said What She Said, produced by Théâtre
de la Ville–Paris, co-produced by Wiener Festwochen,
Teatro della Pergola–Florence, Internationaal Theater
Amsterdam, Thalia Theater–Hamburg, in association
with EdM Productions–Elisabetta di Mambro,
premiered at the Théâtre de la Ville–Espace Cardin,
Paris, on 22 May 2019. It received its UK premiere
at the Barbican Theatre, London, on 10 May 2024.

Performed by Isabelle Huppert

Direction, Set and Light Design Robert Wilson
Music Ludovico Einaudi

Mary Said What She Said

I

1. Mary said what she said because my husband's
   father, Henri the Second of France, got her mother,
   Lady Fleming, with child. He was king, and no king
   was ever a free man. He had eyes in the back of his
   head, but of these two eyes, only one was beautiful,
   Diane de Poitiers. The queen, the evil eye, Catherine
   de' Medici, was as outraged as the beautiful Diane de
   Poitiers that Mary's mother did talk so, did boast so.
   And so they sent Mary's mother home. Let Scotland
   shut her up, they said. Let Scotland be her lying in.
   Let him fill her there. If you ever bed a king, keep
   it to yourself. Mary did not weep, but I did, I wept.
   The king gave me pearls and told me to wash them
   in the sea, knotted strand by knotted strand. I am no
   stranger to the sea. I have smelled it and seen it and
   tasted it. I have even been delivered up to safety by
   the sea. But the only salt water that has ever washed
   my hands or my pearls, wherever they be now, came
   from my own two eyes.

2. Father of France, farewell. He died of a splinter in his
   eye. Death sneaked into his body's mighty fortress
   like a bird come over the rampart, a little thing not
   singing. My father died of grief and this royal grief

made me queen. My mother became sick at sea easily. My mother took me, the girl queen of Scotland, to France. She was so tall I thought men carried her before me, like a statue. But then I never saw her again. I was in France where Henry the Eighth kept no table. He wanted to feed me to England. My mother snatched me from England's kitchen. Arm yourself with patience, she said. And then someone tried to poison my pears. Memory, open my heart. Let the past part my lips. The stars never lie. But how we misread them, bright drop after bright drop in the sea of night.

3. We had begun our journey on the wrong day, that day I was received in Rouen with my mother. It was not the right day, and because of that mistake their birds, a gift to me, all died. They carried us in procession and set us down near the cathedral in a square filled with grass and grown up from this floor were tiny dwellings of straw. This was a village brought all the way from the other side of the horizon, from Brazil. The savages were dressed in helmets of feathers and themselves looked like their huts from Brazil. It had been bread day the day before and the air was still sweet and the morning wind brought such a burning sweetness. The savages were frightened of the bears and the people of the savages and my mother of the feast. (I never saw her again.) Brought with as much care as gold, the birds from Brazil that had been alive

the day before were living no longer. They hunted out a witch and burned four of them. They burned the village from Brazil and converted those of the savages that would, and burned those that would not. And all because it had not been an auspicious day. The priests prevailed upon the people nevertheless to pray for me and never to cease to love me. But it had been the wrong day for this love.

4. Once upon a time I was so white the poets went mad. I was white, white and smooth and flawless. They went mad, I was so fair. They couldn't believe it. They said so. I was just-fallen snow to this one and worked alabaster to that one. I can't remember all the flattery. Star in the heavens, something to aspire to, unblemished, pure, someone to die for. You are the bouquet of your own bouquet, they said. She is so wondrous fair, they said. Her sweet mouth, her eyes in which love must rise victorious. So they said. They would not stop. Fairest of all goddesses. (That one lost his head over me and they cut his head off for it.) But for another poet the sun was too common. In me the poets drowned. They hid under my bed. Is it not insane to write of love? Men make for the cruellest of mirrors. I can see in their shyness how beautiful I was. No, women are the meanest reflection. In their smiles I can divine what I am no longer. They should take heed. Beauty is a tyrant and bitterness is all the tyrant teaches.

5. I had never seen a boy. I'd seen only my husband,
    the new king of France. Poor feverish thing, born
    of the evil eye. What chance had he with her for a
    mother, her heart an innkeeper's book, no better than
    she should be, come, as she did, from a brutal line
    of cheats? What chance did he have in his soft blue
    cloak? Mary said we looked like a pair of bejewelled
    goblets, but one of the eggs was cracked. He crawled
    up the marriage bed like a shadow. We slept, hand in
    hand, slipper to slipper. We tossed bread from Mary
    to Mary. We chased my Marys from door to door.
    He tried to dance, but he could not keep up. He fell
    down in a sweat, rolled over, and cried out. They
    carried him off and he died. No longer Queen of
    France, better I had died in my white widow's dule,
    better I had stayed in the nunnery. But then I would
    never have seen a youth in all God's perfection or
    known a man in all his God-given violence.

6. Mary dared to say what she said because Henry was
    my cousin. She dared to say, Sister in misery, what are
    you thinking of? This is never what I had imagined
    for you, you, with him, like that. A queen is never
    alone. Her privacy belongs to those who must never
    cease from gazing upon her.

7. So it was, before this, but I like to think of them as
    around, and so you are around, my maids, my Marys,
    even you, miserable Mary Fleming. You are here with

Mary Beton, singing and choosing my jewels, and the
two of you are with Mary Livingstone, at embroidery
and ready to laugh, and the three of you have gone
to find dear Mary Seton, who loves me best, and
always has.

8.   His skin slides through my hands, and when I bathed
his neck, I bathed my wrists. I was so white. Better
I had died at sea than marry that beardless head, my
ruin. Better I had eaten the pears from the evil eye
than break free and set sail, queen of that land where
all is fog and rock and urinating sheep and where
all the houses have ridiculous names. Inchmahome.
Peebles. Strathbogie. Even now I can smell the
gamey chamber pots and the wine, the mildew in
the borrowed tapestries and the maggots in the dead
green horses. Scotland dishonoured my brave father.
O it is a shock, a sin, but I do hate Scotland. How
I hate Scotland. I hate France and I hate the Mother
of France, covered in her tomb by worms, her black
heart tarnishing its silver box. (Adieu, adieu, ma
France.) I hate Scotland, but most of all do I hate
England. When I think of England I want to kill.
Had I been born a man.

9.   Go a-hawking then.

10.   Eat fresh ginger, the silly Mary said. Fit for the
beggar Scotland made of me. Farewell, France.
I fear I shall never see you more. Scotland had wood.

The barbarous folk lit bonfires everywhere that could not fail to raise wonderful tragedies. They came to sing. O lusty May, with Flora Queen, her turtle dove for her mate. They sang and sang. They screamed like the savages they were. They called this music. So this was music. Well done, Scotland.

11. I was a bride. Our marriage was proud, though our love was not real. The great had been against us. Mary said what she said because she herself wanted to marry. Queen of the Bean, Mary Fleming was wooed by a wretch. He seemed a man, but he proved a traitor. He was a traitor and he dragged Mary Fleming down with him. She thought of her mother, punished out of France. She betrayed me, on her husband's say-so alone, she who had lived with me and for me all her life. She said they were my letters.

12. I said they could marry, each one of them, every Mary. They were free. They knew my mind then. My time to wed again had come. He was so pretty-waisted. I will save you and you me, I said. The stars we are born under. He loved diamonds and sapphires and to have men scrape before him. He was as pretty as Salome, he who would set himself over me. This Henry was just a boy. My cousin, king of this, my kingdom, your bride Mary is contrary, so take good care.

13. 'Tis true, James, I am married, and have given myself
    to another, and in that act have falsified the promises
    I made you. But were self-interest forgot and
    impartial justice had liberty to speak, you would with
    the surest compassion reflect on the bad necessity
    which forced me to it. France, Spain, England and
    Rome were providing me with husbands; my half-
    brother was depriving me of everything but the name
    of Queen. How but by marriage could I put a stop
    to the solicitations of the one side or have curbed the
    insolence of the other? Well you know it was not in
    my power to make choice of you then, unless I would
    see my crown torn from me, but also to resign both
    our lives to glut the implacable malice of our foes.
    (I did not write this letter.) Think not that it is love
    which furnishes me with arguments to justify my
    choice, for I protest by the same dread power by
    which I have so often sworn that your brow is the
    dearest thing on earth, that it is still, and ever will be
    so, while I have life. (This I wrote.)

14. The boy had pretty legs and pretty fingers and big
    sad eyes and he followed me everywhere demanding
    of me in the most unmanly way anything and
    everything I had within my gift to bestow upon him.
    Twelve falcons, twenty gold horns, his best boon's
    best manor, it mattered not. His slender be-ringed
    hands were always floating just below my eyes. He
    was empty-headed and besotted and he was a bore.

He pouted. He wanted to go through doors ahead of me. The pack of rascals made short work of him. Not a year had gone since his vows, to me, and the rascals of Scotland made him hate me and want to do away with me. Backward country of hounds and jackals, place of hell laid waste with fire and sword. When he thought he had killed me he remembered how much he loved me.

15.   There is nothing more to do here. My prayers are short and frail. He had such beauty, and he had a heart of wax. He would have let the lords of Scotland kill me, but I had my champions. To save my child's life, I smiled at him. He confessed how he got among my murderers and the murderers among my beloved Rizzio. My musician, my confidant, trusted even by Mary Seton. My hated husband confessed, then his tears poured, as water from a bleeding rock. We fled the palace after dark, together, but I could not ride. I was sick with child, his child. We will get another, he cried. I rode after him, and how I rode, hating him, the drunken boy father, the coward and schemer.

16.   Why was I endowed with a soul so little capable of cruelty, yet urged to acts which have so much the appearance of it? Know that what I do, I do for you, for the comfort of your shoulder, for those shoulders, for the thickness of you, James, for the smell of you, a man who can kill.

17.   I am under the tempest of my divided thoughts.
Advise me, comfort me, find some way for my relief.
I have no friend but you. But what is it I am asking?
'Tis dangerous to be loyal.

18.   Never was a soul more harried than mine was that
dreadful night. A thousand horrible ideas ran through
my distracted brain. Sometimes I thought I saw my
husband, the man I made king, all covered over
with wounds and with his dying breath imploring
vengeance on his inhumane murderers. But he started
it. He got drunk and signed my dispatch.

19.   They pretended to be my friends and blew him into
the next world. By the boy Henry's death, I was
indeed once more a queen and again enjoying those
pleasures which power affords, these being chiefly
heartache and more heartache. They killed him
because he would not kill me and then they accused
me of killing him. Only James was true. James, Earl
of Bothwell. The rascals helped him to stretch that
kingly neck and then they blamed him for it. He
made such a sound when he strode the realm as lord
and free man. I was still young. It was too soon for
all to be lost. We had had not much of our time.

20.   When I married for the third time, no one sang.
Good Mary Seton cried. God rinsed my womb
with my child's blood. Henry's child went on living
while James's child died in my tired body. But I was

not sitting on a stone when they took me prisoner.
I was mounted on my horse. My standard flew. Yet
I was become a witch, I, the one and only Mary in
Scotland and the Isles. I was to be defiled, I who had
walked from the Louvre to Notre Dame beloved of
multitudes. Men have died for me by the thousands,
snorting. I did not look when James retired from the
field. Our army had vanished. I could not bear to
think of them cutting his off. I made James go. I was
to forsake and renounce the congregation of Satan,
but it was too late. I like to think of him alive, he
who put his hands on my throat and his thigh on my
mound, a husband, at last.

21. They lied, the pack of rascals. They said my Mary
would be there to attend me. I was made to go alone.
They said she would not come, because I had been
too quick to marry my husband's murderer. They lied.
I had no thing fit for my estate. They took away my
mount. I entered my own city on foot. They uncovered
my head. They showed me their grimy banner of
James Bothwell lording over a dead Henry Stuart
and they said the killing was born of a bad woman's
command. They said a son called out for vengeance
at a father's killing. Murderer's whore, one said and
many then said after him. They brazened their torches
and urged a royal lady to like the flame's lick. They
did not dare to spit in her path, but they befouled the

footsteps she left behind. The women pointed. Burn the harlot of Rome. Their queen walked on.

22. It was my mother who told me the Maid of Orleans heard Saint Michael the Archangel and Saint Catherine of Alexandria and Saint Margaret of Antioch. Saint Michael the Archangel and Saint Catherine of Alexandria and Saint Margaret of Antioch sang to her. If it is your fate to die for the truth it is not vanity to want to hear of it from angels of the best quality, voices from the front ranks, spirits that lift us. We have a right to the company of those angels and saints that break all chains. To command the armies of your self-oppression you must embrace the heritage of the loudest hearts. A dragon swallowed Saint Margaret of Antioch and she made him sick. I could have told Saint Catherine what happens to women who must contend with men in council but she had to learn for herself that her blood is milk. Michael the Archangel gets by with promises. If you are to be pierced by an arrow and not by a man then the Lord's chieftains should hasten through your window, for they have much to tell you, and not enough time. The archer pulls you from your horse. You must become the loudest heart in a great hall.

23. The sun rules the heart. No one had seen it yet, but I felt Venus cross the sun when I miscarried of my child. The armies had not yet joined. We went

[13]

from place to place, restless and lost. Two of
the companions of my old happiness in France
surrounded me, one of these loyal Marys herself
then a married woman like her queen. They watched
unceasingly for any dark body that would enter
upon the disc of light and as they did so I yielded
myself up to the morning. Mary asked Mary which
husband be the father. The sun's image exactly filled
the window between them. They watched from
sunrise, although Venus's motions forbade me to
expect anything before afternoon. Mary asked, for
she thought I could not hear, Is she with or against
God? Mary said it was known at court and abroad
how I had kept myself from the king. Therefore, it
was Bothwell's child, and got when the pretty king
was alive and drinking. During all this time Mary
and Mary dared to pity their queen, I was awash
in the sun. Mary and Mary thought I did not hear.
I could hear a whisper as far away as Jerusalem. At
fifteen minutes past three in the afternoon, the clouds
dispersed, revealing the lip of the moon, and I was
once more invited to the task of living. I then beheld
a most bloody spectacle. A perfectly unhappy shape
emerged from me and as it did so something fully
entered upon the Sun's disc, so that I sensed that the
limbs of Mercury and Venus were precisely coincided.
Far away false Mary was telling stories of masses
sung at the palace for the devil.

24. I am the relentless, delicate storm that folds men. Mary told me at last she had me for a witch. She thought so in France, when I made the birds die, song upon song. I am the dragon and its smoke.

25. The evil eye hated me because she had nothing to teach me, nothing I wanted to learn. I was born queen and did not want lessons in holding my tongue or keeping my head. Catherine hated me because I wanted to study the ways of Diane and I did. Learn that beauty is a storm and in blasted weather men will resign their will as well as their reason. See how I have learned everything from her and nothing from that eye that conjured Saint Bartholomew's night. Because men love me and have always loved me, hateful women think me a witch. Let them know then there is delicacy in my witchcraft. Men take me for their cause. I am the silk. Sing hay trix, trim go trix, under the greenwood tree.

II

26. To have seen me riding from parliament in the midst of men, having the royal crown upon my head, the sword and sceptre borne before me, is to have been astonished.

27. So it was before this, but I like to think of them as around, and so you are around, my Marys, even you, miserable Mary Fleming. You are here with Mary Beton, singing and choosing my jewels, and the two of you are with Mary Livingstone, at embroidery and ready to laugh, and the three of you have gone to find dear Mary Seton, who loves me best, and always has.

28. Mary Fleming's mother liked to dance. That is when the king first saw her. She danced tolerably well. Catherine de' Medici danced not at all, so weighed down was she by her jewels and tails. She trusted no one with her strong boxes and wore as many of her jewels at one time as she could so that she would know they were safe. One of the rings she wore looked as though she had made a ring of one of her victims' heads. A page had to stand behind her and hold her hand up. She never danced. Mary's mother was triumphant. That is when Diane de Poitiers taught me how to dance. Gestures descended

from Caesar's favourites. By the time the king had tired of Mary's mother I could dance the hawk gliding between cliffs. But Diane de Poitiers. She alone danced the tragedy of the woman who needs no partner.

29. The lords of Scotland had me fast. The prisoner queen. But my friends got me away. We rose and fell. We rose, but fell to nothing. We could not hold one bridge over a single shallow stream. I turned away. I had to. The lords of Scotland could not catch me. I was too fast. An English escort waited for me. But my heart was safe. I'd left it with James. No one would rise up for me any more. Elizabeth Tudor had fed everyone from her cold dish of English gold. And rather would Mary in a dungeon lie than live at large where falcons cannot fly.

30. For whom do you fringe and tassel in gold this purple velvet cushion?

31. I must confess that I am grieved to the heart by the crosses which I have to endure, but especially by the estrangement of my son from me, and his being set against me. But I pray to God to let me die rather than learn for certain that such a thing can be.

32. I am ashamed to be under the necessity of representing to you so particularly my miserable situation here, but the evil presses me and constrains me to declare it to you.

33. I thank you most affectionately for the trouble you have taken, since your departure from this kingdom, in giving me news of France. This has afforded me singular pleasure, as I receive but very little intelligence from any other quarter. I shall ever feel, both in thought and affection, deeply interested in the weal and woe of that crown, as it is my duty to be. So bring the moon.

34. I will tell you that I am in a walled enclosure, on top of a hill, exposed to all the winds and the pettiness of purgatory. Within the said enclosure, resembling that of the wood of Vincennes, there is a very old hunting lodge, built of timber and plaster, cracked in all parts, the plaster adhering nowhere to the woodwork, and broken in numberless places. The said lodge distant three fathoms or thereabouts from the wall, and situated so low, that the rampart of earth which is behind the wall is on a level with the highest point of the building. The sun can never shine upon it on that side, nor any fresh air come to it; for which reason it is so damp, that you cannot put any piece of furniture in that part without its being in four days completely covered with mould. I leave you to think how this must act upon the human body. It is rather a dungeon for a base and abject criminal than habitation fit for a person of my quality, or even of a much lower unfortunate.

35. I will tell you of the letters I wrote and the letters
I did not. A queen must sign many letters, and a
woman write some of her own. I will tell you of the
letters I wrote and of the letters I wish I had not.
Let me swim to Greenwich and search the letter
books and take mine out – or is she at Nonsuch
with her council, that crawling, worming pack of
hellhounds. The injustices hatched against me. Men
belonging to Morton, Athol, Lindsay and Glencairn
lifted their dressing at me as I was conducted against
God's command and my order to the evil courtesies
of Lochleven Castle. They were Bothwell's enemies
and showed themselves to him, me, as did their
ancestors before battle. I was removed to a closed
wagon. I should have bared my breasts and blinded
those clansmen. I should have converted them into
church marble. I had to appear weak, but I promise
you I was not. I would have written no appeals had
I known how much she wanted my heart turning
over an open fire.

36. As to the article bearing the confirmation of the last
treaty made at Edinburgh in the month of July, you
may condescend to the allowances thereof. These
instructions are given to our reverend father in God,
our trusty counsellor and ambassador to our good
sister, to be used with the advice and concurrence of
those who are sent in commission by our lieutenants
and nobility. May our good subjects be joined with

our ambassador in the treaty to be made with said
good sister. It is for the appeasing of all unhappiness
and the contracting of further amity between us.
I have from her as tokens of good will a Psalter and
a Book of Hours. I send by wheel carriage in return
the last French portrait of me.

37. My bastard brother told me a great secret of
statecraft. It is never too late to blame someone else.
He snorted on his fist. Very well. I snort on my fist
and blame the ambassador I sent on my first coming
into Scotland. He stank of wet hides. He smelled
like my uncle the cardinal and that is why I put
my trust in his sense. Of which he had not enough.
He offended England and incensed Elizabeth to
disquisition about the very matter she has never
forgiven because it cannot be forgotten. She would
ask me to undertake not to hinder her children. My
ambassador, being a man, rusted not enough on the
point of that, as she had no children, and he did
say that was a business of no great weight. A hush
overcame the chamber. Her fool farted. Elizabeth
withdrew. My fool was forbidden the old maiden's
court. His horses were turned out of Windsor unfed.

38. Little miserable rooms and excessive cold and
tapestry that I have made and night that I did not
make. Next winter on horseback.

39. Send me the headdresses from Poissy and other
     things as soon as you can. Your mistress and very
     good friend. I have heard of his arrival over there.
     Your mistress and very good friend. I shall render
     him every service. I shall write on the arrival of
     my secretary. I shall not forget them. Your very
     good mistress and friend. I have made some new
     regulations. I have commanded my brother to
     write to you. I have had a frightful dream from
     which I awoke fully convinced of that which was
     subsequently confirmed. I beg you will write me a
     particular account of everything. I send you a letter to
     be delivered. Your very good mistress and best friend.

40. Your most affectionate and obedient. Your very
     affectionate good sister and cousin. Your most
     faithful and affectionate good sister and cousin and
     escaped prisoner.

41. Dismiss from your mind and manifest the contrary.
     Censure a prince and save a life. Cast me out and
     recover my honour. Accept this kindness and lead
     me falsely. What I here tell you is enough to satisfy
     you. Procure for me some new fashions of veils and
     send them without fail to my good sister. They say
     she is a bonfire needing only an ember. Find her
     on a progress. She pays royal visits to her subjects,
     saves her money, and bankrupts her lords. She can
     go where she wants. I was very glad that she was

pleased to receive the sweetmeats. She must pay my household. We've embroidered fields for her. Let us not act any longer in this capacity.

42. She detains my horses and even my mules. I paid two hundred and eleven pounds for ten horses. I paid drink silver and bridle silver for ten hackneys. Wait. To maintain the peace within, we must wait. Dismount. Everyone. I have been put off with words long enough. It is time for my actions to answer my words. They will tell me where I stand. What place is this? I can smell my uncle the cardinal, but where am I?

43. I have not been a little confirmed by the accident of the priest who, after having been grievously tormented, was found hanging from the wall opposite my window. His mouth was moving. We could not understand. He had news. He had news from Kent. He had news from Ghent. They broke up mass in my chapel, disturbed the choir, and the clerks left with bloody ears and my priest carried his own broken head. How do I talk of some other thing or not dwell on my misfortunes? I see achievements of honour, borne by heralds, and eight bannerols, borne by esquires. Mary could read, but it never did me any good. We parted without tears.

44. I bob up and down on granite and chalk. I must find something more steady. I crawl. I climb. I close

my eyes deep in the yew and listen to its centuries.
I can hear the doves and waterfowl escape without
packing. My surprise that I am fluent in falcon. In
this tree I am the terrible truth.

45. I remember Monsieur de la Mothe. He was so
intelligent. He laid his chin on my knee when he
knew that I was by mournfulness possessed. I think
of his eyes. He was patient. We starved together. His
flaxen coat grew dull and then fell out completely.
He was pink and cold and I wrapped him in the best
I had. He died noiselessly.

46. If the Cardinal of Guise, my uncle, is gone to Lyons,
I am sure he will send me a couple of dogs. And you
must buy me two more. For besides writing and
work, I take pleasure only in all the little animals that
I can get. You must send them in baskets, that they
may be kept very warm.

47. Puyguilhem was as jealous as any man. To pet
Mauvissière I had to shut Puyguilhem out of sight.
I think someone drowned Bess. Jean they found
frozen and I believe Bertrand was cooked and eaten,
I do. Monsieur de Glasgow and Madame de Briante
both lived a very long time, though she became
as ill as her mistress who adored her and taught
her French. She never answered to English. Prince
Labanoff sleeps between my feet, hidden from the
world. I am your shelter, little one.

48. Salute me and speak. Have you had commands from
     Elizabeth Tudor to use such language to me? Is Mrs
     England in her kitchens? Have you had orders from
     my brother to use such language to me? Stay. Is Mrs
     England in her pots? You are not as low as you can
     go. Her council declares her genius greater than that
     of Saint Tutilo. Have you had orders from my son
     to use such language to me? Loch to loch they run.
     Would I ever take by unlawful violence the crown
     from the head of my own son? Glen to fishy glen. If
     he does not wish his mother's love, he can have her
     throne. It is made of stone. My mother sang.

49. I am prepared and booted. Sign, sign. Let us journey
     to France. Hold my ships in readiness at Dover. Then
     carry me over. Yes, carry me over. The wind was so
     favourable that after embarking we found ourselves
     happily arrived in port and in the road of Calais that
     same day at one o'clock and, thank God, without
     any seasickness. Lord Father and Mary my mother,
     I dream. I eye dangerous dreams. When, when has the
     wind favoured me?

50. Kiss my hand. I am condemned to know who and
     what I am at all times. In my lying down and in my
     rising up. As for me, born a sovereign queen, who
     sought refuge in this kingdom upon the assurance
     and promise of friendship, they wish to make this
     imprisonment drive me from affliction to affliction

to the very last, as if it were not sufficient that, after seventeen years of my life spent in such misery, I have lost the use of my limbs, and the strength and health of the rest of my body, and that various attacks have been made upon my honour, but they must persecute me in the bargain, and say isn't it wonderful, the waves were not real. In which case, there is a pebbled shore in my chambers where I remain, fearful of all consolation.

51. I conjure you. My countenance will be unappalled when I come to what is two foot tall and twelve foot broad. What I will come to will have a railing all around and be covered in black. The stool will be black, the cushion on the stool will be black, the block will be draped in black. I will hardly notice, I, the one and only Mary in Scotland and the Isles.

52. God grant me the patience. I am holy and worth keeping.

53. I have been so strictly guarded during the last eighteen months that all secret intelligence failed me down to last Lent, after which time it was too late to fight like wolves. My brother ran among the swans, at his age.

54. They came yesterday, Monday, out of spite, and took down my canopy, saying that I was no more than a dead woman, and without any rank.

55. My coach I leave to carry my ladies and the
horses which they can sell. I will that my houses
at Fontainebleau be sold. I will that my estate of
Trespagny be kept for my cousin de Guise, for one
of his daughters, if she should come to be married.
I must be quit. My order must be annulled. I, having
received nothing, say this. I will that my accounts
be audited. I will that my treasurer be paid. To my
scholars, two thousand francs. Five hundred francs
to the hospital. Take my physician into your service.
Do it this day. Tonight I will write it again. The Will
of the Queen of Scots. By candlelight. Every week
I write the Will of the Queen of Scots. It is a demon
in the road. The Will of the Queen of Scots. Every
week I must move it. This burden, in my road. There
is no room for the smiling pleasure and cheerful
countenance of the demon of wax seals. I could say it
passes the time. This great instrument from my hand.
It passes the time.

56. May I have my ladies to attend me? He answered
me like this. We fear that some of their speeches
or behaviour would grieve your grace and prove
troublesome to us. Your ladies would not stick to
put some superstitious trumpery into practice. The
dipping of handkerchieves into your blood. I am the
married Queen of France and the anointed Queen of
Scotland, and he will not grant me the courtesy of my
best ladies, my apothecary, my surgeon, and one old
man to attend me in my steps before my last steps.

57. Since my last to you, herein enclosed, kept ready ever
     since the beginning of last month, fresh restrictions
     have been laid on my liberty and I am refused
     permission to write to the Queen of England, my
     good sister. I am astonished beyond measure at
     this proceeding, knowing in my conscience how
     little occasion I have given for it, having taken
     particular pains, during the whole of the past time,
     to accommodate myself as much as possible to
     all that I thought agreeable to the said queen. I
     urgently require of her some declaration concerning
     her intentions regarding my said new restrictions.
     If I cannot write to her, I request you to undertake
     the office. Such harsh treatment greatly impairs my
     health. My good sister forgets the past, her past,
     thinks not of the future, the future of her realm, and
     believes only what she says when she is in council
     and may do all the talking. Her council is theatre and
     there cannot be shown her own ancient history as
     a princess declared illegitimate, writing to her royal
     sister, in despair for her neck.

58. That I am queen cannot be put on or taken off like
     a cloak. I am my Estate. This evening I do not tire.
     Outside, it is trying to snow. The moon is large and a
     pale blue. I have no earthly judges in this light.

59. I forgive you with all my heart, for I hope this death
     shall give an end to all my troubles.

60. In honourable custody, the Queen of Scotland and
    England's heir, prisoner-guest of gossips, what am I,
    and of what use is my life? I am a vain shadow. My
    future is a living death. I wanted everyone to read
    that. The whole world wanted me free. Set her free.
    Her Majesty must renounce, the ambassador said.
    The painted Virgin who led (leads) men through her
    back door, she made me over. I will die rather than
    ask for pardon and the last words of my life shall be
    those of a Queen of Scotland.

61. It is an insult, to be forgotten like this, to be looked
    at like this, to be watched over like this, to be
    gathered around, like this, to be soothed, like this.
    I terrify myself when I am calm. What sounds are
    those? What are those voices? But I can't wait. I am
    going on. I hear them, I know they're there. What
    a sacrifice. Be silent. Mary said what she said. They
    bolted doors and dripped wax over everything.

62. Jezebel corrupted him with hunters and hounds.
    I sent my boy a monkey. The Prince of Scotland sent
    it back.

63. The struggle not to laugh openly is great. And then it
    is over too soon. James would not have music.
    Our quiet was the thing that told me we were
    doomed. His head cocked, he listened for sounds
    of approaching enemies. I am queen. Only one man
    has ever heard my singing. He was toothless in my

arms and would not remember now anything of our short acquaintance as son and mother. I sang with my mother. I sang with my nurse. We sang every day, and we sang for hours when it rained.

64.   They had the dagger, I had the dance.

65.   Mary is a lady bright,
      She has a son of honour might
      Over all this world she is light
            Bona natalicia.

      Mary is so fair and sote
      And her son so full of bote,
      Over all this world he is bote,
            Bona voluntaria.

      Mary is so fair of face
      And her son so full of grace,
      In heaven he makes us a place
            Cum sua potencia.

      Mary is both good and kind,
      Ever on us she has mind,
      That the fiend he'll us not find,
            Cum sua malicia.

      Mary is queen of all things
      And her son a lovely king,
      God grant us all good endings,
            Regnat dei gracia.

III

66. The Holy Ghost taketh from women all power over man. Let women keep silence in the congregation. Gorgeous apparel is odious in a woman. Dost thou not know that thou art Eve? Because death entered into the world with her. And therefore, I say that this monstriferous empire of women be openly revealed to the world that some may repent and be saved. But this Knox could not take his eyes from my neck. Let not the book of the law depart from thy mouth. But this John Knox fixed at the pendant I wore on my royal breast. To promote a woman to bear rule is repugnant to nature and contumely to God. He tried not to bow when he came into our presence. He stood aloof from my welcome, and yet the low thing stood close enough for me to smell his last five meals. The Devil wears Geneva bands.

67. Men declare that Scotland was under the practice of a crafty dame. Scotland drank of the enchantment of Circes. I am led by something strong. In my end is my beginning.

68. Elizabeth Tudor slashes at her serving women with knives. She produces terrible odours when she eats.

She has sores on her legs. Yet she'll send to the Tower
any man who does not sniff her up as the queen
of heaven. Elizabeth Tudor never wanted to meet
me face to face, because she was afraid (is afraid)
what I would (will) make of her afterward. It is the
insolence of her joys and banquetings that I cannot
bear. She proclaims her body unmolested, while
I am the raging of women's madness that must be
repressed, I, the one and only Mary in Scotland and
the Isles.

69. So it was before this, but I like to think of them as
around, and so you are around, my Marys, even you,
miserable Mary Fleming. You are here with Mary
Beton, singing and choosing my jewels, and the two
of you are with Mary Livingstone, at embroidery
and ready to laugh, and the three of you have gone
to find my dear Mary Seton, who loves me best, and
always has.

70. The painted virgin believed the Catholic Plot, her
own spy's concoction. Every highborn Catholic boy
within riding distance of my prison was taken out of
his father's house and put to the rack and strapped
on a hurdle and driven to his martyrdom. They
made me watch once, long ago. My brother made
me watch. He held my face against the window and
my arms behind my back. I, his queen. I heard the
thump, the splintering of wood. I heard the people

gasp as one. My brother shook me. The executioner
had missed his mark. I heard him moan. The people
called out his courage to him. I heard another thump.
I could not open my eyes. The people cheered him. I
opened my eyes. They rushed forward to be stained
by some of his blood.

71. Let each look to himself and see what God wants.
They deserved life, those boys. Mary said one youth
begged for an angel to come down to comfort him,
he was so afraid and in need of a sign of holy favour.
One day his tomb will be a place where miracles are
performed. They have died by their thousands for
me. Love your queen and you will be exalted even
as she is.

72. On leaving Calais we saw from our white galleon
another ship strike a sandbar and sink too quickly
for anyone to save the mariners. The day was very
still and we could hear them in the confusion. They
called to God, and some called out to their mothers
to save them from the swirl. It was over so soon.
The surface of the water gave no hint of what had
happened. When I die, let the seas be disturbed. Call
up the ghosts. I am going home to my mother among
the stars.

73. In Rouen our barge glided under a bridge and
directly we had passed out from it the parapet fell
and dropped some merrymakers in the river. I saw

a row of them as though they had made to bow
to a river god. I saw the backs of their heads and I
heard the hum of them in their surprise. It is always
a surprise. The hooded figure in the throng is always
a surprise.

74. It is His Majesty's will that all be laid waste with fire
and sword. Burn Edinburgh and raze the city to the
ground, as soon as you have seized whatever is worth
taking. Plunder Holyrood and as many towns and
villages as you can. Ravage, burn and destroy Leith,
and the same whithersoever you go, exterminating
men, women and children without mercy, wherever
resistance is shown.

75. Ten thousand were killed at Pinkie because of me.
I never knew, until Mary told me. The English had
come to take me to London for their boy prince.
I was five years old. I did not know. She said she
would make me see reason. I have caused the death
of so many. What glory. Now I cannot walk.

76. Sir, good King of France, by my cousin the Queen of
England I am after twenty years at last condemned
to death. I would that after my death my body
should be transported, into your realm, where I have
had the honour to be Queen of France. I am to be
executed tomorrow, as a criminal, at eight o'clock of
the morning. I have not had leisure to make you a
full discourse of all that has passed, but if it pleases

you to credit my heartbroken servants then you will
hear the truth. God be thanked, I despise death and
in good faith protest that I receive it innocent of all
crime. I acknowledge no trial or jury in this realm,
of which I am the heir. The Catholic religion and the
maintenance of the right God has given me to this
crown are the two points of my condemnation, and
yet they will not let me say that it is for the Catholic
religion that I die, but for the fear of change to their
own. They have been very instant with me to receive
the doctrine of their minister summoned to that end.
The bearers of this letter will testify of my carriage in
this my last act. It remains that I beseech you, ancient
ally, who have ever protested your love to me, that
at this hour you give proof. Recompense my broken-
hearted servants, according them their wages. Pray
for a queen who has been called most Christian and
dies Catholic, stripped of all her goods. As for my
son, I recommend him to you in so far as he shall
merit, for I cannot answer for him. (I have never seen
my son walk. It has been that many years of trouble.
God has decreed that my son shall not remember his
mother's face.) I have the hardihood to send you two
stones, rare, for the health, desiring for you a happy
and long life. You will receive them as from your
most loving sister queen, who dies giving you witness
of her good heart towards you. I recommend to you

again my servants. My Lady Mary Seton is here. All France remembers that she has been with me through life, ever since my sainted mother brought into my service four little maids of honour, each named Mary.

77. I lead the Dance of Death. She who holds the stick owns the cow. But I lead this dance. London plans a revel for my severed head. Let no one lie about how well I did. Let Mary's face be full of grace. Mary has a son. The painted virgin leaves no trace.

78. There is no one to my left or right. Where is the pack? I hear only the wind in my ears. The sky is streaming as I tilt the clouds. The treeline dances. The rest of the landscape throws itself away. I am so far above the ground. I move so fast. I am moving so fast, I am not real. They love their queen. I am a straight line. Men are amazed. She is a true prince, the only Mary. I am the surprise. Farewell, France.

79. Whereas it has pleased Almighty God to call to His mercy our late sovereign, the lady, once upon a time, Queen of Scots, so styled, and hold here. I bark yet.

80. I am well far from that step, I tell you, and I am no leftover. I never signed that one, the act by which my crown was turned like a bowl on to my boy's head. If he ever gave thought to me. The silence is not the worst of it.

81. You are the bastard child of a ditch digger. You live in a cave. You want to eat me. Try my dog first. I make a gift of it to you, Sawney Beane, Sawney Beane. I can still sing.

82. My son will forget me and run you down with bloodhounds. He will find your cave and your floor of rising bones. Bennane Head, Bennane Head. He will scrape you until you become a skull. I will not die like you, pulled apart, cut up, and burned. The one and only Mary in Scotland and the Isles.